Mom,

I'm sorry we are living in these terrible times, But thank you for being witness to this.

THE CLOCK THAT TOLD MORE THAN TIME

and The Concept of "Human"

Corey Friedman

Bloomington, IN Milton Keynes, UK

AuthorHouse™
1663 Liberty Drive, Suite 200
Bloomington, IN 47403
www.authorhouse.com
Phone: 1-800-839-8640

AuthorHouse™ UK Ltd.
500 Avebury Boulevard
Central Milton Keynes, MK9 2BE
www.authorhouse.co.uk
Phone: 08001974150

© 2006 Corey Friedman. All rights reserved.

No part of this book may be reproduced, stored in a retrieval system, or transmitted by any means without the written permission of the author.

First published by AuthorHouse 9/20/2006

ISBN: 1-4259-5977-6 (sc)

Printed in the United States of America
Bloomington, Indiana

This book is printed on acid-free paper.

dedicated to

   those who

disagree

Table of Contents

Foreword ix

Prologue xiii

Introduction xvii

Chapter 1: Physicality 1

Chapter 2: Interactionism 17

Chapter 3: Abstractions of Rational Thought 37

Chapter 4: Individuality 45

Chapter 5: Life 51

Chapter 6: A Meaning of the World Around him 63

Chapter 7: He Who Believed In An Idea of Time 71

Chapter 8: Nihilism and Adaptation: Fun Suggestions for Saturday Night 79

Chapter 9: Acclamations of Truth, Untold Lies of the Social Machine 88

Bibliography 97

Foreword

Corey Friedman's book, whatever the fuck it's ultimately going to be called, is a great big sprawling mess. In fewer than 30,000 words, Friedman cartwheels through centuries of epistemological enterprise, busting thousands of pages of philosophical exegeses into sentence fragments and bringing them face-to-face with the most humdrum human realities. In this book, John Locke sits to sup with Pauline Kael and St. Thomas Aquinas. Somehow, it almost works.

I wouldn't call this a "great" book, or even a "good" book—it's *not* a "good" book, in the way we usually understand such things, and I don't think the author would disagree. Tell you what, though: This is a *damned interesting* book, and that's a promise. It's one of the strangest little screeds these peepers have ever peeperized, and reading it will probably do wonders for your mental health.

Technically, this is a book about philosophy, but it's not going to teach you anything about that. This is also a book about being human, but it's not going to tell you anything you don't already know about humans. And this is a book about self-perception, though it is unlikely to dent your own.

This book works what magic it has in areas far removed from its own subject matter. It is *not* a book about curiosity, but within its pages—in its hectic explanations, in its relentless topic-jumps, in its frenetic repetitions of certain key points—you can find out everything you ever needed or wanted to know about the emotional realities of honest inquiry, and about what a harrowing experience the search for knowledge can be.

I've known Corey Friedman for far longer than I've understood him, and the longer I know him, the more I like him. People seem static at first glance. Their attitudes and beliefs and reservoirs of knowledge seem like fixed, natural facts, beyond the power of individuals or circumstances to alter. And with some people, this perception is perfectly accurate. With Corey Friedman, it is not.

Corey Friedman is one of the very few people I have met in my life who is as righteously confused by the world as he ought to be. He is unspeakably upset by the incredible difficulty inherent in trying to get a grasp on this weird miasma, and he is eternally scrambling to catch up.

In my more romantic moments, I feel that this is the single most important trait a human being can possess. Ignorance—and the acceptance of ignorance—is the only real evil that's ever menaced the good people of the earth, and it's people like Corey Friedman who stand in its way. He is continually scrambling after information, constantly in search of Truth, and he possesses no belief too precious to alter, should new information come to light.

This book is a product of his manic search, and the speed and enthusiasm of the writing is a brilliant example to anyone currently languishing in the intellectual doldrums. From time to time, it has more in common with the paintings of Jackson Pollock than with the writings of, say, Immanuel Kant, but this is only appropriate. We are all just children, here—there are few giants in this age, and too much wisdom has been acquired in too many places over the long centuries of human speculation for anyone to stand a reasonable chance of catching up. Corey Friedman's search is a frenzied one, and this book captures that frenzy well. If you just keep turning the pages, following Friedman as he lopes after glimpses of insight and discovery with all the dumb grace of a young beagle chasing a rabbit across a freeway, it is my belief that something of the passion the author has brought to his subject matter will be transferred to you, the reader. That's the power of the word, and that's the power of art.

– Brandon Kenneth Thorp, June 27th, 2006

Prologue

"To the ones I love: I'll stand by you. To the ones I hate: I'll bury you."

- Anonymous

I began this book as a philosophical journey. And just as with the beginnings of all philosophical journeys, there was only one thing on my mind—getting closer to the truth. Finding out something about something that no one knows.

I have written here on numerous aspects of existential thought, and originally, that was all I wished to do. Throughout the development of this text, however, I began to see that this goal was becoming less and less attainable. Various twists in my own life, a few infusions of weird humor, and a masochistic taste for self-mortification has brought this text to its present form.

The finished version of this text took a lot of time, and would never have been possible without my editor, Brandon K. Thorp, who is (as of this writing) also the Editor In Chief of *The Mogenic Free Press*. Brandon has provided me with numerous insights, and without Mr. Thorp's gainsay, neither I, nor this text, would be of the quality it is today. Brandon is the type of person who giggles in the face of tragedy and snarls at seriousness. Mr. Thorp is one of the most brilliant minds the world has yet to see, but I have a feeling that will change soon, thanks to this book, which explains everything about everything. It will make giants out of dwarves, and pit bulls out of pugs.

I would also like to thank Casi Davis. If not for Ms. Davis, the cover of this book would be extremely dull. Casi was able to capture the sentiment of this book in one photograph. To me, that photograph—the cover of this book—is extremely special. Casi drew every inch by hand.

I would also like to extend a special thanks to my friends and family for always sticking by my side. They are the very foundation of what "1%" means.

For the reader: I would like to clarify a few things. First this text is not a textbook on existentialism: It is a collection of ruminations on existential thought, and underpinned by information imported from other areas of philosophy.

I would advise the reader to have fun with this text, if possible. Fun may not be an option, for, as we shall see, sometimes philosophical inquiry will result in bleak answers about bleak situations, and a certain amount of fortitude is required to take this seriously while remaining whole and happy. See where your life is at when you begin this book, and see where it's taken you by the time it is through (approximately forty minutes later). Whether its impact is great or small, time will have passed, and you will have changed.

While this text was being composed, I encountered a great many people. Some have come and gone, while others just stuck around. Indeed, I cannot seem to get rid of some of those fuckers. They have all taught me something that I have tried to incorporate into the following chapters.

This is a book about life. It's a book about human tragedy, and moreover, it is a text that that will hopefully guide the mind of man through the miasma of modernity.

But *who is* this modern man? Is he a creature we primitive primates have yet to see, or is he another happy fiction of contemporary intellectualism—an illusion? I'm going to suggest that "modern man" is a myth. He is nothing but a tamed primitive, doing primitive things in a primitive concrete jungle of his own devise. From the gutter to the skyscraper, man takes credit. But is credit really due? Did man build these things of his own volition, or is he simply a manifestation of the higher, blind will of nature?

Keep that question in mind.

With that said, I thank you. Hopefully, this text will provide you with some abstract notions on the nature of "man" and what is to become of him. Take the time to discuss it with your colleagues. Most of us do not know the meaning of life, but one thing is certain: Life's a learning experience, and if it isn't, it sucks.

Regards,
Corey Friedman

INTRODUCTION

It stood there, looking at itself in the mirror—a reflection was all it saw. The thing gazed deep into its own hazel eyes, and they were staring back, avidly, into its face, and then its mind, and then its soul. Soul? Was the person-thing staring into an idea of itself to which it was accustomed, or a physical construct, definitively formed? In that moment, the person-thing realized something: He realized he was a human, and he realized that he did not understand anything at all.

Cold sweat dripped from his wan, silly face, and ran into the sink below. And just as the first drop hit the marble, his understanding began to evolve.

Angered at his futile grasping towards knowledge, he ripped at his long brown hair, separating chunks of flesh from his scalp, his raw nerves meeting the cold air. This was something that could be understood, at least—pain. Plagued by brain-bound bio-chemicals that he couldn't control, his body was wracked with careening, unfathomable sensation. Physiology was no abstraction, now: It was real. Tears filled his octal outlets, and soon he could taste their sweet salt on his lips. Now, he felt alive.

Possessed by these demons, existing *a priori* in his being, Samuel realized that he had unleashed them from the depths of his very consciousness, where lived his life itself.

What does it mean to be human?

Throughout all of human history, humans have sought to produce some explanation for their condition, and their interpretations of their observations have varied. Existentially, epistemologically and ontologically, different theories of what it truly means to be human have been continually expounded over the centuries. It's a question that has consumed individuals for lifetimes, and it remains unanswered. That the human mind is capable of understanding such a dynamic and abstract question is obvious; whether or not it is capable of answering such questions remains unclear. The prospects aren't great.

From now on, we will not refer to *"What does it mean to be human?"* as a question, but as a concept unto itself—the "concept of the question." This is a kind of synthesis, and it is part of an environmental approach to solving one of life's paradoxes.

Some state that existential questions like this are best left alone, and that is probably true for certain individuals. Living pay-check to pay-check, or in a blast crater, does not lend itself to epistemological abstraction. Some assert that the concept of "meaning" varies from human to human, and this is certainly true as well. As science is good for producing answers, philosophy's strength lies in producing challenging questions.

Over the course of his life, a man may ask himself, "Do we live to die?"—a question that opens an existential gateway, leading to questions like, "What is the purpose of being human?" and "Where is human existence headed?" and, most famously, "Why do we exist?"

These are all questions that have manifold answers, if they have any. Most are justified, in one way or another. That we have, thus far, failed to reach consensus about our conclusions is proof enough that none are satisfactory.

"We identify our existence and we understand that, whatever it means, we are *Human*. We have the Latin *humus* for soil and we have the Greek *hamai* for ground, or earth. Both these words look to their common origin the truly ancient Sanskrit word, *hsam*. It seems our long-ago foremothers and forefathers were quite in touch with their humble, earthy origins."[1] So, as we see, the origin of the word *human* is consistent with the evolutionary and—dare we say?—*biblical* perspective that humanity's origins are earth-bound. Primordial soup, if you will, "Dust + God's Breath − Rib". Anyway: The inorganic made organic.

Humans are earthly in their derivation. However, in their machinations, humans display an apparent autonomy and freedom, which seem to belie that earthly origin. The dichotomy between the brute, physical realities of human, corporeal existence and the complexity of human consciousness is the terrain inhabited by all of the greatest philosophical problems.

Kant posits that human beings are creatures of choice, whereas the "lower" animals are creatures of instinct, and this certainly appears to be true. From a human perspective, at least. As the albatross of humanity's grubby history is lightened by the unending progress of modernity, our slimy origins recede farther into our memories.

Another great polychotomy exists in the conflicting conceptualizations of humanity proffered by all of the world's prevailing worldviews—there is the biblical, the scientific, the belief in intelligent design, the humans-as-cosmic-orphans paradigm inhabited by the deists, millions more. Humanity's earthly origin is virtually the only belief held in common by all of the competing

---

[1] http://www.baltimorechronicle.com/human.html (sic)

theories (we wisely exempt the Scientologists, and their Magic Volcano, from this assertion).

From an evolutionary perspective, these facts may be relevant: Those who subscribe to a Judeo-Christian philosophy would describe humanity as being created in the image of God—this is referred to as *imago dei*. The bible emphasizes "stewardship"—the role of human beings as caretakers of the natural world, to hold dominion over the earth and be fruitful.

Understandably, humans are made from the same fundamental elements as the earth. A human understands those elements, and has made use of his environment by creating the technology with which we live, and which facilitates the growing abundance of human life on earth. Humans have changed natural materials to suit their needs. A human must use these materials so as to sustain a homeostatic environment, bodily, which then stimulates homeostasis on a macro level.

This book will be a guide to understanding *what* a human is, not just *who* a human is. Throughout the book, the human may be referred to as "he", as is my choice. Please know that the term is meant androgynously. This text also attempts to dehumanize the human, and therefore it is a deconstructive text—so be warned.

This is not a handbook for the human on how to be human. Rather, this is a text that precedes those issues, and deals with basic assumptions about the things we take for granted, every day—the commonalities in our existence. I believe the reader should also understand that this book will not give a direct answer to the question of what "being a human" means. This text summarizes others, and suggests another angle from which to approach that question—human existence and understanding.

It is imperative that we understand *what* the human is and *how* he exists, and investigating these questions may shed light on *why* he exists. Just as the human has changed his environment, he attempts to make sense of his perception of reality. He justifies his life. He invents or discovers ideas that make him live comfortably and give meaning to the world around him. As we shall see—and, if you're reading this, as you have most likely already observed directly—the human invents or discovers ideas that help him cope with reality. We would hope to do better.

The human conceptualizes, understands and thinks. He is an enabled being. The human is different from other organisms in this way, but in every other way he is virtually identical to all of his fellow species. Objectively, his life is no more meaningful than that of an amoeba. The human interacts, thinks, has a sense of individuality, and he encounters emotion—which, subjectively, seems utterly magical. Whether or not we use the human invention of science as a tool to explain emotion—as, say, the product of chemicals and synapses working side by side—or if we merely accept them as miraculous things, springing up in the course of everyday life, we still attempt to make sense of, attach to, and identify with emotions. That seemingly-simple process has been at the root of humanity's search for meaning, thus far.

The things that the humanoid cannot quantify are too often left to religious or metaphysical explanations. That is because there are certain things—events, coincidences, or anachronisms (events which lack explanation during the era of their occurrences—say, early hominids witnessing a meteor shower)—that the human cannot make sense of. He tries to adapt or make up an answer that will best fit his needs, throwing the unexplained into a theistic junk pile. Today (and always), the human is contemporarily sophisticated, but relatively ignorant. There are things in life for which he has no explanation, and which will remain mysterious until some point in the future. One cannot have tomorrow's technology today.

The human is a creature of concepts, and can only make sense of life in the way that best suits him. He will never know the purest truth, but rather, will only know what he has invented and explained. He considers evidence and makes assumptions. This is the positivist approach, and it works well, though it is eternally unfulfilling. Uncertainty lurks at the heart of truth, for in the most objective way, we can never apprehend what "truth" is. We only know that it should exist, somewhere.

Do we really have a reason to live? If so, what is it? Is it a sense of personal advancement? It is the human who has given himself a definitive value—made things like "advancement" meaningful—but because that value is so utterly reliant upon a prejudiced, human perspective, it can never be fully explained. Indeed, the appeal of most of the world's great art is found in that art's inarticulate striving towards just such an explanation.

Humans modestly accept the condition that they are fallible. Flawed with hope and desire, the human accepts that he is doomed to fail his own ideals. He rarely accepts the fact that he is only flawed because of his own, circumscribed concept of "fallibility." Without his particular and arbitrary set of ideals, man might, in fact, be perfect.

The concept of "sin" usually gets in the way of such grandiose epiphanies. For the human to accept that he lives with sin negates the idea that the human may very well be a form of perfection. To those living creatures that are not fortunate enough to have been born human, perfection is irrelevant—or a given.

We exist in a world with no colors, sounds, smells, or tastes. Our perception of reality is very far removed from an objective perception of the actual objects that inhabit the real world. Our senses provide us with an interpretation of what reality is, and it is through that interpretation that we experience the whole of life. But there is no guarantee that our perceptions are accurate at all. Nevertheless, we cling to it—and we explain our clinging to life in a million different ways, though it may ultimately be a result of nothing more than an ingrained, biological imperative.

This book is my ideas converted into text. If it were not for you, the reader—presumably, also a human—this book would be useless. This text is a medium through which I have the ability to convey my thoughts to you. The chair, bed or bench you are sitting on is only a chair, bed or bench because you think it is. It is important that you start thinking in these terms so that you can identify the reality you inhabit more accurately. That chair is someone else's transubstantiated into wood, metal or plastic. From idea to object; from intangible to tangible.

It would not be weird to think that you are reading my thoughts (that was the idea), but on the other hand, it *is* a little weird to think that you are sitting, driving, eating, wearing, or speaking someone else's idea. The human's ability to convert his ideas into a vast number of objects is just another characteristic that we overlook, but which makes us profoundly different from the rest of the species we dwell with. He is not just living in his environment; the human *is* his environment.

Despite his profound aptitude for altering his surroundings to suit his needs, humans feel an equally profound longing for a higher rationale for his own existence—and, lacking any such ready-made rationales, humans tend to invent their own. These ideas bypass (and predate) scientific inquiry, and exist on the much shakier terrain of the metaphysical imagination. Nevertheless, even these dreams are the flotsam and jetsam of rapid-fire, meaningless physiology; we boil down our philosophies to synaptic snaps, crackles and pops, and suddenly, Jesus is just a chemical that took a wrong turn near the medulla oblongata.

Nevertheless, knowledge progresses, despite our over-arching need for a higher rationale. One pulse at a time, a thought is born, the imagination is unleashed, and with centuries, reality begins to reveal its foundation to the curious—a foundation so phenomenal and magnificent that the very thoughts which allow its apprehension are made out of the same stuff as the ground we walk on, and the lightening we dodge.

The Human Imagined—and that was the catalyst for all we see around us. It is humbling to think that no other creature has so self-consciously altered his natural habitat. To recognize our remarkable feat, it is imperative that we recognize the contrast between our origins and the world we currently inhabit.

Chapter 1:

Physicality

Today, Samuel knew he would have to challenge the world. He knew he was about to do something that lots of people weren't going to approve of. Over the past couple of days, Samuel's hazel eyes had turned obsidian-black. Where he had desperately ripped his hair from his scalp, only deep maroon patches of clotted blood remained.

His ivory skin was now stained with dirt, and the mirror that had led him to understand his nature now lay in hundreds of pieces on the floor. One of these pieces, Samuel knew, would determine his fate.

The sharp edges looked so appealing, yet they made Samuels stomach turn sour with grief. He reached for one of the shiny, jagged shards and felt it touch his once-warm, now-clammy fingers. As Samuel hefted the thing and brought it closer to his wrist, his eyes began to change back to their original color and his stomach ceased its churning.

Samuel could not do it to himself, he realized—he had to live for tomorrow. Tomorrow, he knew, would justify his existence today.

The identity of the human exists in many forms, but exists, in essence, beyond the trappings of those forms. He exists without skin color, religious bias, creed, social class, or sexual orientation (though, clearly, he exists *with* these things, as well). The human is a walking, talking, breathing, self-contained, thinking and responding product of the ground on which he walks. He is a product of the earth; a freak of nature—and, ultimately, "human" is a word we slap on anything that meets a particular set of criteria. This chapter will examine three different forms of human interaction: His interaction with himself; his interaction with his environment; and his interaction with others like him.

When the human comes to invent either an idea or a physical object, that idea or object is made manifest in the world around him, forever shaping the received realities of his fellow humans. For the human's every action in the modern world is inspired by the ideas of man—the next time he goes to lie on his couch, or uses the restroom, or brushes his teeth, he is doing so with the aid of another human's idea, now made physical.

Couches are not immutable facts of existence, nor are toilets. The word, one might say, has been made flesh.

Man understands, with his protoplasmic mind, that he is a relatively able creature (we make obvious and loving exceptions for members of The Walmart Worker's Union). Man understands the ideas and concepts of omnipotence, omniscience, and omni-benevolence—and just because he cannot realistically aspire to these ideals, that does not in any way limit his adoration for them. He automatically assimilates these ideas with a *ne plus ultra*, and then calls that hypothetical structure "God". Though little to no empirical evidence exists to suggest the existence of such a being, we hold desperately to the notion that perfection exists, somewhere.

It may seem too obvious a point to belabor, but let it be said: The human exists in two basic forms—the male and female. Each of these accents, compliments and corresponds to the other, and together they form a union of nigh-uncanny harmony (sometimes) and complexity (yea gods, always). Sadly, perhaps, there is no evidence to suggest that this union has any greater meaning than the sum of its parts. On the evidence, it is possible to conclude that life is a void, and that the importance of procreation is based on no higher motivation than the survival of the human genome. Love, romance, family, friendship, fellowship: All manifestations of biology, doing its thing.

Male and female coexist side by side, hand in hand. From humanity's intellectual interaction arises a form, a "wave of energy," perhaps, which associates/congregates human beings based on criteria involving similar thoughts and ideologies. If humans are simple, procreative beings, such congregations (like religions, nations and the Kiwanis Club) fly in the face of the species' very purpose: Breeding. It stands to reason that, if there is no higher purpose to humanity's existence, then there exists no compelling reason to not live hedonistically and selfishly, so long as it makes us happy.

We must not do this. We cannot allow man to live life with the absence of law, order, or a sovereign to protect the weak. Nevertheless, we understand that happiness is subjective, and varies sharply according to who is defining it. The human is a cultural, conceptual creature, built on self-generated ideals and driven by amorphous inspirations such as hope and love. Our natural alignment to these ideals is illustrated by the concept of human rights.

Simply stated, human rights are improvable—and as "natural facts", they are almost certainly lies. They've served a function, thus far—they are the concepts which keep the idea of order intact, and help human societies avoid chaos and unnecessary meanness. This is serious work, because the universe's natural state, *sans* humanity, is chaotic (from any perspective greater than that of an electron).

But the universe functions well, it seems, and has done for billions of years. So why is it that humanity strives to change and govern every aspect of his environment? Why all the *micromanagement?* Is he scared of himself? Is he trying to create an environment that is sufficiently stable for weak creatures to get ahead and reproduce? And *why?* If the weak are weak, why not let them fail?

If the human animal has natural rights (life, liberty, freedom, happiness, property, etc), then what happens when one person can only savor freedom by infringing on the rights of another? *How's about a little love for the serial killers and cannibals?* All of us, to one degree or another, utilize the resources at our disposal to get ahead, succeed, and achieve happiness. This is the understanding underpinning libertarian philosophy. So—what if a given human's future happiness is dependent upon the destruction of another? I briefly mentioned this problem in my first book, *Iconoclast: Contemporary Comments on the Human Condition.* These are all paradoxes which show the logical fallacy inherent in such a system. So-called "natural rights" (rights given to man from a deity, or from the cosmos, simply because he is human) have been proven over and over to be nonexistent unless enforced by a government or manmade institution, such as common law. So, one may conclude, the development of these rights (enforced by man-made institutions) is facilitated by governing bodies for the sole purpose of organizing the populace and maintaining the premise—entirely artificial—of stability.

Man is male and female, black and white, and is further defined by infinite other variables. Freud described him as a "psychosexual" being, and invented classifications and qualifiers beyond counting. Society has given him a personality and decreed that it display itself in his physicality. His phenotype used to be defined by his genotype, but now even this is subject to change. And it is understood that all of the fundamental changes wrought upon the nature of human identity are presaged by arbitrary societal determinations of what, in any fleeting instant, is most desirable.

> "To live is to act. We feel, we reflect, we experiment in laboratories—but we don't stop there. We go on to appraise issues, to make decisions, and then to move. And as we appraise and decide we make reference not only to scientific knowledge but much more extensively to 'knowledge'—however fallible and arbitrary—deriving from faith." [2]

The intuitiveness of the human and his penchant for invention—the invention of both himself and his environment—is motivated by a hunger for personal gain and nothing more.

---

[2] Wheelis, Allen. The end of the modern age. Basic. New York. 1971

But, to be human means to be comprised of tiny mechanisms that do not have the ability to realize themselves within the greater context which *we* apprehend (and spend most of our lives ignoring). Tiny machines—proteins, cells—making bigger machines, which in turn go on to make still bigger machines. From the macro-molecule to the amoeba to the rocket scientist to the . . . ? We are all made from tiny mechanisms that do just what they were designed to do, with no higher ideal in mind than relentless cell replication. All of this wondrous organic machinery that helps the human live is all working in the interest of creation and nothing more. These mechanisms are autonomous, yet are constricted in their self-awareness and productivity in ways that they can never understand.

To write endlessly on the physicality of a human being would be a pointless task. From observing the variety of phenotypes which can be derived from the human genotype, we can see that said genotype can only be accurately described as amorphous and everhanging. Basically, human physical characteristics are manifold, and depend on a great number of factors, a few of which are:

1. Parental Genes
2. Birth Defects
3. Physical Accidents
4. Substance (drug) induced changes

5. Current fashion
6. Environmental factors

And the list could go on and on. The human ages in a manner consistent with the natural laws to which he is forced into unwanted aesthetic contemplation. The immutable laws of speed and math and physics do not age with time, though our subjective understanding of those things grow with continuous discovery. The human can travel hundreds of miles per hour through his understandings of the brute mechanics of "speed", yet no matter how old he is or what level of technological development he has achieved, that same speed will exist. The human is affected by time, but time will never be affected by him.

The effort for the human to maintain a definitive stance on the unchanging verities of the universe surrounding him is an effort fraught with inevitable disappointment. Humanity's grasp of natural law is in a constant state of flux, and while certain, basic laws may be known, the finer intricacies and implications of those laws are undergoing continual change and refinement. Nowhere can this be seen more clearly than in a careful examination of life's ultimate origin.

There was a time, not too distant, when the finest minds of Europe and America were in basic agreement that the world sprang into existence some six thousand years ago at the whim of a great big bearded Jew in the sky. This concept has fallen out of favor amongst the Smart People of the world, but has yet to totally disappear from the public consciousness. The human conceptualization of life's ultimate genesis is an idea that is still undergoing continual metamorphoses. At the moment, the most comfortable compromise found between those who adhere to the Big Old Jew hypothesis and those who favor Darwin's version of natural selection is called "Intelligent Design".

Intelligent Design is a theory that could be explained as a hybrid between creationism (the human being created by a higher power) and evolution (the human being is what it is because of the continual process of natural selection). The principle of I.D. is that, yes, humans could very well have been designed by a higher being, but that the mechanism through which this design was and is continually implemented is evolution.

> "Evolution embodies information in every part of every organism. A whale's baleen embodies information about the food it eats, and the liquid medium in which it finds its food. A bird's wing embodies information about the medium in which it does its work. A chameleon's skin, more dramatically, carries information about its current environment. An animal's viscera and hormonal systems embody a great deal of information about the world in which its ancestors have lived."[3]

---

[3] Dennett, Daniel C. Kinds of Minds: Toward an Understanding of Consciousness. Basic. New York. 1996

We now will come to a critical point in the text where we need to deal with the idea of future man. What will the future human be like? Idle contemplation—or even non-idle, rabid, frenzied contemplation—of concepts like "evolution" and "creation" and "intelligent design" do little to provide us with a viable hypothesis as to the future of the human genotype. When asked about that future, common responses from early 21st century college students include:

> "Future man will probably look the same as contemporary man, however technological advancements may be developed to alter or enhance man's physical characteristics."[4]

Interesting comment. However, since we know that the contemporary man has changed in physical characteristics from what he was a million years ago, it may be safe to assume the we are caught in a slowly changing phenomena that alters our phenotype-by-way-of-genotype.

Technological advancements may lead to post-birth superficial alterations, but there are no retro-genetic consequences of a face-lift or liposuction. Botox fucketh not with DNA. It could, however, be argued that there is a possibility of some future geno-drink that may inhibit or alter the genotype of the individual, which will in turn affect his offspring. Growth hormones that are

---

[4] Survey Answer.

injected into natural foods are also contributing to the alteration of modern man. Modern medicine is keeping the human alive for increasingly lengthy (and depressingly less productive) periods of time than ever before. The extension of life is a feat perpetrated by future old men to sustain the ideal of what he presently believes life should be: Painless and long.

Dietary consumption is another factor that may contribute to the slow-paced alteration of the human genotype. A question to consider might be: "What will future man eat, that is different from contemporary man?" Technological developments have imposed rapid changes upon the biosphere of the planet, and these changes may have long-term results which are, at this point, impossible to predict. Humanity's food supply may be altered, and various genotypes may be increasingly favored in the milieu of competitive reproduction. An answer to this question will certainly give us some idea of what we can expect our descendents to look like.

Anthropologists have shed a great deal of light on the history of our species, and we now know for certain that there are vast differences in body size, skull size and walking capabilities between *homo Neanderthalus* and *homo Australopithecus*, to pick an example at random. There is no reason to believe that progress has ceased because we now recognize that such progress exists. Evolution is not a game of "Red Light, Green Light."

> "Well, man is very adaptable to different environmental changes, and that's what has made our existence so fruitful and long. But with adaptability comes some changes, maybe to adapt to global warming, etc."[5]

This response demonstrates a common misunderstanding about the nature of natural selection—the belief that outside forces somehow influence a creature's genetic make-up in a direct way. In all probability, those who will be at a genetic advantage in the event of cataclysmic global warming will be those who, simply, through some accident of genetics, happen to have an ability to metabolize food more effectively (which will be necessary due to less irrigable, fertile soil), who have a higher melanin content in their skin (to deal with increased solar radiation), or those who can breathe underwater (due to large portions of the human population suddenly finding that their picture-perfect suburban neighborhoods suddenly sixty feet below the surface of an inland sea). Picket fences—least of all *white* ones—are not water-proof. Indeed, they have proven to be pitifully inadequate defenses against raging tidal waves in nearly every instance in which this question has been put to the test.

---

[5] Ibid Survey.

"These individuals thus confronted the environment by generating a variety of actions, which they tried out, one by one, until they found one that worked. They detected that it worked only by getting a positive or negative signal from the environment, which adjusted the possibility of that action being reproduced on another occasion. Any creatures wired up wrong—with positive and negative reinforcement reversed—would be doomed, of course. Only those fortunate enough to be born with appropriate reinforcers would have an advantage. We may call this subset of Darwinian creatures *Skinnerian creatures*, since, as the behaviorist psychologist B.F. Skinner was found of pointing out, such "operant conditioning" is not just analogous to Darwinian natural selection; it is an extension of it: 'Where inherited behavior leaves off, the inherited modifiability of the process of conditioning takes over.'"[6]

Man has adapted, though in genotypal terms: This adaptation has been unwilling and unconscious, and though he dwells in the moment, one would hope he understands the importance of future inevitability. Man is coming into an era in which he possesses both the desire and the ability to alter the course of his own evolution, freed from the constraints of Darwin's blind natural selection (and this, too, is evolution).

---

[6] Dennett, Daniel C. Kinds of Minds: Toward an Understanding of Consciousness. Basic. New York. 1996

"Races will become dissolute."

If you have ever seen the *Matrix Trilogy*, you may have noticed that there are few Caucasian people standing in the sacred underground city of "Zion". There is a reason for this. Many people, including the Wachowski Brothers, believe that there is a possibility that, with the advent of widespread interracial relationships, there will eventually come a point at which there are an insignificant number of racially pure-blooded individuals living on the planet.

There is a belief that we will soon exist in a uniracial society. It is demonstrable that the contemporary tendency towards interracial coupling advocates the destruction of all races that indulge in this type of nontraditional procreation. The dilution of races slows down the process of human evolution, as significant changes to the human genotype can only occur within small populations.

Viewing both sides of this situation, one can see that there are both positive and negative consequences of this genetic dilution. First, we can see that the traditional image of man will be abolished, leaving a bland, homogenized "neo-human" in its place, without access to any of the traditional breeding-grounds of culture (ethnic identity, etc). Cultural diversity will be found only in history books.

Whether or not the "equality" question would be made moot by this blending remains unknown—although it is almost certain that, human nature being what it is, we'd find some non-racial excuse for being mean to each other. The idea of equality itself stems from the assumption that man is divinely blessed with "natural rights." Race-mixing will be considered a blessing by some, while others will think it disastrous. This is almost certainly a contemporary concern—in a world where everyone is brown, no one will take the time to question his or her own brown identity.

"Man will overcome his flaws."[7]

As it patently observable, we are coming closer and closer to an age in which parents will routinely alter the genetic makeup of their unborn children so that those children fit some idealized aesthetic or intellectual profile. Hair color, eye color, height, IQ—all will be customizable. Science is reminding man of his own hard-wired weaknesses while striving to eliminate them in coming generations. Science has hardly yet made itself equal to humanity's long list of frailties, but progress in this regard is inevitable.

Over the past several centuries, science has improved the conditions of human life so profoundly that he can longer understand from whence he came. The edu-

---

[7] Ibid Survey

cated human can discern the difference between the living conditions of the contemporary and those of antiquity through study, but he still lacks a gut-level understanding of the reality of the deprived conditions under which his ancestors labored. Similarly, it is probable that future man will view our existence as having been primitive and difficult. We might envision a future man with few of the problems that plague us currently, but future man will doubtless have his own set of problems, which we cannot presently predict.

"Man will be smarter."[8]

There is no doubt that today's man possesses more knowledge than those who walked the earth before him. He builds on the species' accumulated knowledge, and now even the stupidest among us are keenly aware of facts that would have been hopelessly abstract to our ancestors.

Man, in the future, will not be the same as man today. We are talking about our offspring, our kin, but they are not us. Nor should they be.

---

[8] Ibid Survey

Chapter 2:

Interactionism

Samuel was supposed to die that day, but something, maybe a misfiring of a synaptic switch, led him to put the piece of serrated glass down. His life was endangered no longer. Samuel had defeated fate, the same fate that guided him through every breath of life from birth. Now he was free, and nothing was going to change that. Samuel was free of whatever metaphysical restraints had held him down. Now he was real. Not just his body or the things he could sense, but his *ideas* were real. His mind was wandering widely, exhausting the rest of his body and beating his emotions into sick submission. Every step Sam took was another moment with the power to steal his breath from his lungs.

The human begins at a period known as *Tabulla Rossa*—the clean slate. His future is decided by the subsequent stacking of experience upon experience. The human experiences reality through interaction with those like himself (other people) and those unlike himself (coat hangers, blue whales, transistor radios, etc). Death is the end of cognitive interaction between two circumscribed objects (the human and his environment). When death takes over, all that remains of that particular human's essence does so in the memories of those who witnessed his existence, and in whatever physical legacy he has left behind. It is by thinking in terms of such interactions that the human can justify his life and understand its nominal value.

This is somewhat arbitrary: The human interacts and coexists with other species, and often exploits those species for personal gain and survival. He seldom judges his worth in terms defined by those species.

Humans, with rare exceptions, live in groups and societies, and we can see how, consequentially, values are created on the societal level. Human society has put in place ideals of perfection and beauty that create a powerful need to "achieve," by certain definitions of that word. What we get as a result, in addition to smooth-functioning societies, are psychological disorders, such as anorexia and bulimia, which are socially created. These come about as a result of the dichotomy between societal values and those values that would be most beneficial to the individual as such. The vulnerable and the weak are crushed, and the lucky are elevated.

Humans are peculiar, for they have invented the social anomie that they dwell in. Social characteristics have resulted in psychological necessities: I need that new car! I need to fit in!

These social indulgences tend to guide the naïve human spirit, and infringe upon his natural abilities to guide and judge from any kind of meaningful, individual moral perspective.

The human began communication with gestures, then advanced to sounds and finally to the words that make languages: The humanoid put together phonemes and made them into words that represent universal ideas to particular humans—and, having done so, he communicates constantly.

The human, through language and the ideas that language is capable of communicating, has an unconscious grasp of the underlying process of interaction. He who is mute, deaf, dumb or blind is known to have a handicap—a relative handicap, making him less able to function in his community. He is handicapped, in essence, from being effectively human.

Man understood the need to congregate. Man discovered, through trial and error, how to effectively form a society, or a social union with many members. Man then agreed to give up some of his freedoms in exchange for protection, to live with a lingering presence of protection—even those who do not possess the qualifications by which man first came to create such societies.

The human ages with time.

The human dreams throughout the night.

The human perceives a world around him, although he is unable to experience it directly. Man's perception of the world relies on man's senses, which are, we know, entirely fallible. Man knows the world around him from what his senses lead him to know. His senses provide his only available description of the world he lives in. Thus, man is a slave to his senses—and, over time, becomes quite blind to their peculiarities.

Is it possible for man to travel through time, and is it possible that he has been doing so ever since his creation? We say no, seemingly oblivious to the fact that we time-travel every night. When I go to bed at time X and wake up at time Z, I have traveled straight through Y, but to me and my perception of reality, it feels and seems as though Y didn't exist. Although I was alive for those 9 hours, 10 hours, 15 minutes, whatever, my cognition was stolen from me (or given up), thus effecting human time travel. We don't think about it, but it happens every day—we are such slaves to sense that we are almost pathologically ignorant of its defects and quirks.

The Clock That Told More Than Time

Why does the human interact, and with whom does he do so? Human beings were, so far as we know, the first animals to engage in an intensive intellectualization of socialization, leading primitive, organic and instinct-based social groupings—families—into complex, hierarchal clans and advanced societies, like our own. The birth of the complex social order led to the formation of the social contract, and the invention of "rights."

These rights (man made, natural, or God given—depending on how you approach the situation) are designed to protect man from himself, cushioning primitive animalism in a bubble of ideology. The dominion of such thinking is very limited—hurricanes are decidedly uninterested in human rights, as are rabid wolves.

In order for the human identity to survive and prosper, he must procreate and he must advocate the proliferation of his own identity. Anything contrary would be anti-humanistic. The human survives on the products of his land and nothing more. He is born into a world of manmade ideals and concepts that he will have to live his life by. Some would ask, "Are we pawns of history?" More often than not, the answer is "yes." It is not uncommon for the human to be used as a tool. Slavery and human ownership have been around since the beginning of man, and there are none among us who are not beholden to forces far larger than ourselves.

> "What is alien to the spirit of man is not the machine itself, but the vision of mechanism, the dreamlike insistence that the universe and all that it inherit, including man, is nothing but a machine, and is thereby knowable as an object, as a machine can be known." [9]

Man wants to understand his interactions with the world around him. He wants to justify those interactions, and he wants to control them—for he is a modern creature and accustomed to freedom, and he does not like that idea that he is not in control of his life. Nevertheless, he is beholden to all those whom have come before him. His interaction with himself depends upon his self-image, as it relates to a world created by hands other than his own. He climbs up or down within the social hierarchy, attempting to control his destiny, almost universally oblivious to the fact that the milieu in which he operates was created by creatures besides himself.

It is not uncommon for man to be solipsistic (Latin for "myself, alone"). "Solipsism" is the idea that I (myself) am the only person who is capable of thinking. Everything around me is part of a machine, programmed to interact with me in a particular way. Intellectually, we

---

[9] Wheelis, Allen. The end of the modern age. Basic. New York. 1971

know this is a silly thought, but our behavior reflects a solipsistic understanding of the world as often as not.

> "I am a philosopher, not a scientist, and we philosophers are better at questions than answers. I haven't begun by insulting my self and my discipline, in spite of first appearances. Finding better questions to ask, and breaking old habits and traditions of asking, is a very difficult part of the grand human project of understanding ourselves and our world." [10]

Perfection is only an aspiration. The mortal strives to achieve it, knowing it is impossible. Man lusts after technology, believing it will bring him close to perfection, neglecting to see that technology can also be devastating. Man optimistically lives his life under the aegis of "progression." Though contemporaries may be stuck in their ways, those are not the ways of their parents'—and future generations, too, will change with the times.

It is the prospering of the human, and the resultant advancement of science that has led, on one level, to a functional explanation of the world. But it has also led to the demise of the world he knew.

Bioethics is a field concerned with how the human can properly end or alter his existence and the existence of those around him, including future generations. It

---

[10] Dennett, Daniel C. Kinds of Minds: Toward an Understanding of Consciousness. Basic. New York. 1996

is because of human endeavor that the pressing of a button can end all that we know and bring humanity a crashing end.

What is the motivation for humanity's continued endeavoring under the banner of progress, in spite of the increasing stakes? Simply, it is individual autonomy, coupled with an insatiable desire for a better life. These are the primary motivators that have brought us to the present day, in which we have the ability to self-destruct at whim.

Why would a human be made or created with the ability to call a halt to his own existence, and that of all of his fellows?

Why is he capable of executing this process?

How is it that he is able to discern his own destructive potentiality?

These are complicated questions of morality and politics, which exist entirely beyond the scope of our present project. It is useful, though, to make a few observations along these lines. The ability to draw such distinctions between notions of "creative" and "destructive"—the ability to place value judgments upon various manifestations of "progress"—stems from dualistic ideas of good and evil. These are negative and positive categorizations which man has foisted upon himself. By drawing upon our skill in dealing with abstract concepts, we are able to hypothesize idealized concepts of human interaction, and then, when comparing those concepts to a dualistic apprehension of the world we have created, we almost unfailingly classify ourselves as "destructive", "evil", "negative." The kingdom of ideas it at war with the kingdom of matter.

The human uses what he knows to his advantage, but has difficulty in imagining the long-range consequences of his actions.

Humanity is the problem with humanity.

This gives rise to the question: *How could one eliminate the total problem without eliminating the subject?*

Socialization, indoctrination, and the selective use of lobotomies limit human interaction, but could, conceivably, bring about a world that is frighteningly close to what most of us imagine Utopia might be. Marx, Hitler, Stalin—all were Utopians. It is the conflict between opposing ideologies which brings about our greatest trials and travails and keeps us a firm distance from realizing Utopia—but it is this constant conflict which stands as the truest evidence of our fundamental freedom.

Utopia is a place that can only exist within the human mind. The unborn human is naturally a stoic; once he is sprung from the vaginal cavity it is the society that instills his weaknesses—namely, emotions at odds with the raw, pragmatic environs with which he is suddenly surrounded. Misery ensues and Utopia evaporates.

The human species, so far as we know, can only live in an environment that he has the power to change by making his thoughts manifest. Our entire infrastructure is merely the reflection of an idea, or a group of ideas, which have come together, through human ambition, to constitute "the world." The human is a creature who has been shaped by his environment, but equally and dominantly the human has shaped that environment. He has been shaped by his environment to the point at which he came to the realization that he must *do* something about it. He built infrastructure, put men on the moon, made the automobile and formed governments in the interest of his kind.

One of the things distinguishing the human from other animals is his apperception; his ability to conceive of himself. For the human, there is a difference between the idea and the feeling. For example: He has created markets to express his need—or desire—for consumption, acknowledging that it is beyond his ability to make all necessities available to himself. So he relies on others to provide for him, in correspondence with his willingness to compensate in return. It is perhaps humanity's unique apperceptive abilities which enable him to drum up the empathy necessary to conceive of such notions, enabling markets, and thereby modern societies, to exist.

> "Movements attract misfits. The desire to change the world usually corresponds with

personal unhappiness. The frustrated man, not the self-contented one, goes about altering his surroundings. He would do better changing himself, but egomania prevails and fosters a less rational cure for his troubles."[11]

The human has discovered universal concepts, like "math," and has synchronized them with science (science, as defined as "the body of knowledge thus far accumulated by humanity about itself and his surroundings"). He has begun to understand the world around him in a meaningful sense, and has begun to construct a model of the world as it existed before he was born into it.

"Synchronism," the idea that new epistemological connections can be formed between formally disparate ideas, is illustrated effectively in observing the vastly different methods human beings have, in various eras, attempted to satisfy the same fundamental needs (Where does life come from? It comes from God! From penises! From sex! From eggs! From DNA!). The advancement of human beings' intellectual processes makes history a very hard thing to know, and humanity's ideological, emotional, and intellectual origins remain obscured behind a scrim constructed of our own contemporary views.

---

[11] Flynn, Daniel J. Intellectual morons: How ideology makes smart people fall for stupid ideas. Crown. New York. 2004

Humanity has advanced itself in terms of technology, and thus we live in a technocracy. Ask yourself: "Would there be an idea of modernity, or modern technology, without humanity?"

It was the human who was naïvely unable to understand the long-term effects of inventions and innovation. The human now lives in an era of rapid technological progress, defined by Moore's Law[12]. Humanity has civilized itself, and thus we live in civilizations, blessed with order, plagued by anomie.

We live in this idea of an ordered technocracy governed by plutocratic influence. The relative wealth of a society determines the pace of its technological development. It complements our ordered state. Our technocracy exists in a state where we can only have the technology of the present because anything different would result in a philosophic paradox. As a result the human *has* created the idea of modernity, that self-conscious apperception of progress from a primitive past to an ordered future.

I would like, at this time, to re-emphasize that humanity's creation of technology is an instance of the human animal obeying its natural impulses. It could be said, then, that technology is natural, and that it is a part of the human's evolutionary process.

---

[12] the computer that becomes obsolete monthly due to the shrinking and compounding of tiny electronics

The Clock That Told More Than Time

A Biblical Paradox of Temptation

What follows is a logical argument of deduction. The human has an ancient text, but does not know who wrote it. Nonetheless, all religions have at their core a similar text, or texts. The Bible is written in such a way that it requires interpretation, either literally or metaphorically. The Paradox of Temptation goes as follows:

1. God created everything on Earth, including Adam and Eve, correct?
2. God created the Garden of Eden, correct?
3. God told Adam and Eve not to eat the fruit of the Tree of Knowledge, correct?
4. God must have had to create that serpent and the fruit because they existed on this earth only by virtue of statement 1, correct?
5. God is omniscient (all knowing), correct?
6. Eve, when approached by the serpent who encouraged her to eat the fruit, saw the fruit was "pleasing to the eye" and decided she wanted to eat it. Correct?
7. By virtue of statement 5, the human acknowledges that, if God is all knowing, then he knew what the outcome of the situation would be (this limits free will, and is part of the basis of the Calvinists' "Limited

Atonement" and "Total Predetermination" doctrines).
8. So then, why did God knowingly create a situation in which Adam and Eve would be expelled from the Garden of Eden?
9. From the moment of the Expulsion, humans were, according to the Bible, prone towards corruption and sin. But God knew that would happen and God made us that way.

So, by virtue of this argument, would it not be correct to deduce that God is, by human moral standards, Not a Very Nice Person?

Initially, so they say, God desired a good life for Adam and Eve. Then, for some reason, he introduced temptations that corrupted the human with sin. Would this mean that God abandoned his original design for the universe? God knew he made the human with hedonistic tendencies, and because of this, Eve found that apple (which God created) appealing enough that her desire overcame her fear of God. Was this a test that the humanoid failed?

If so, this would mean that human nature is corrupt, and that creation did not work out as intended. But the real contradiction comes into play when we understand the idea of God as an omniscient being. Couldn't it be said that with the temptation flaw, God should have known what the outcome was going to be before he put the context into play?

Of equal importance to these questions—which, as Martin Luther understood, are of grave cosmological import in a world based upon a Judeo-Christian understanding of reality—it is genuinely imperative that one understand not just how the human communicates and understand others like himself (and others unlike himself), but it is important that one understands how the human entity interacts and comes to know the extended world around him. I have included a brief synopsis of the theories of how the human comes to understand reality.

The Illusion of Reality

Reality is not as it seems. This text will explain how reality is not as we perceive it, and how most people are indifferent to the notion that they experience the world only through their senses. I will prove my point by examining how people experience reality through sensory perception alone, using concepts of Naïve Realism (or Direct Realism), The Representational Theory of Perception, and Phenomanalism. Throughout the text, I will explain how the world actually lacks color, sound, taste and smell—how, in actuality, these are simply constructs of the brain.

Scientists and philosophers have shown us that light is not as we perceive it, but particles (photons) and/or light waves that are measured according to the density of their wavelengths. Sound is not sound; it is vibration in the air, excited particles to which our eardrums respond. The idea of tactile sensation is false, as it is commonly understood—what is real is our ability to observe the energy emitted from an object in the real world with our kinesthetic sense. Taste, as one knows it, is the brain's decoding of inert chemical information being transmitted to certain sectors of the brain by way of miniscule electronic impulses emitted from the tongue—a process very similar to the one by which our olfactory nerves decode "smells." All of these senses send synaptic messages that our brains decode to allow us to partially experience the world around us. If there was a gap or a break in the chain of synaptic messages used to translate reality to the human ego, we would be unable to experience reality as we know it.

Have you ever asked your self the question: "How do I know if the color in front of me looks the same to someone else?" It's a question that has plagued the human mind for thousands of years, and our best answers are not good enough for the curious. We can only observe that humans are all made in a remarkably similar manner, in that most (with the exception of the handicapped and congenitally stupid) possess all of these senses, and have learned to utilize them in nearly identical ways. Logically, one can deduce that, since humans are all made similarly, we all experience reality similarly—at least, in terms of sensual perception.

Naïve Realism is the philosophic idea that reality and perception are the same— which concludes that our sensations and physical reality are also the same. This is a common-sense, positivist approach to understanding the world around us. The idea is identical to "Direct Realism," as Direct Realism posits that, "when I perceive reality, what I perceive is the external world."

The human comes in contact with objects in the extended world, and we can agree that our perceptions of them are probably similar. But how accurate are these perceptions with relation to the objective truth of the object under observation? These objects possess characteristics that can be translated by human senses, but the human is a slave to his senses, because he relies solely on them to know the world around him. If there is higher or greater truth to the object than that which is relayed by the senses, a human will always fail to apprehend it. It would have been useful to Marie Curie, for example, to be able to observe radiation emissions beyond the visible spectrum.

The "Representational Theory of Perception" opposes Direct Realism, and states that humans or sensory animals do not have direct access to the direct object itself, but rather, direct access to what is known as a *sense datum* (something that exists in ones mind). This theory is very practical and gives a very precise template or structure to understanding how one comes to observe and experience the extended world.

"Phenomanalism" is the belief that perception is very largely divorced from reality. And while this argument may be fun in philosophical circles where the "Evil Genius" argument is tossed around like cocaine-coated confetti, it has few practical uses. It is impractical to believe that all sensory perception is a mass hallucination that has little to do with objective reality.

All of these theories stem from the assumption that objects possess different qualities (a logical assumption, being that a chair is qualitatively different from a hammerhead shark). These qualities can be divided into two groups: primary and secondary. Primary qualities are those qualities which actually, objectively exist in the real world (the hammerhead shark has teeth; the chair is manmade). "Naïve Realism" and "Direct Realism" both theorize that the direct experience of primary qualities is possible. Secondary qualities are those which we directly experience—the human "decoding" of smell, taste, color and heat, as well as other, more abstracted secondary qualities (figure, extension, solidity, mobility).

Philosophers like George Berkely contend that there are no material objects in the world at all, and that God's world has no color, smell or taste. But there are problems with this idea. How does a physical phenomenon cause a mental phenomenon? The idea also fails to take into account that subjective experience—like "taste"—is "real" phenomena, as much as anything else.

Philosophers such as Locke agree that the human exists dualistically. The idea of dualism was made famous by Rene Descartes, who posited a mind-body dualism. Descartes contended that the human was made up of the mind (the *Res Cognita*) and the body (the *Res Exstensia*), and he viewed the body as the mind's extension into the outside world. It was the body's senses that experienced the world and translated these experiences to the mind. A view like this seems to assume an automatic dichotomy between perception and reality.

Ultimately, it is the philosophy of "Realism" that seems to serve us best, by allowing us room for the fallible nature of our senses, while still acknowledging that a better method of perceiving reality has yet to be developed.

Chapter 3:

Abstractions of Rational Thought

Like many who had come before, Samuel came to be haunted by his skepticism. He could no longer discern whether he was living in reality or a dream. It felt like a dream, but he couldn't wake up.

The past and future fell away and were made irrelevant in the swirling urgency of the instant—a single moment, rich with infinite potential for creation or destruction, seemed on the verge of revealing itself. Samuel felt ready to explode out of himself, out of his world and body and mind, into some unimaginable screaming freedom. He was terrified.

"In the classical Greco-Roman culture man was viewed by the philosophers as being in harmony with nature, while modern Western man often imagines himself in conflict with the status quo, forever combating obstacles to progress and pleasure."[13]

Human emotions tend to infringe upon one's rationality and the ability to think in a certain way. Why was the humanoid created with this weakness? Does it make him more humane? Did he evolve this way for any good reason?

All human beings are created with this same flaw: The experience of emotions which damage humanity's ability to live rationally, and yet which define all of the most important aspects of his existence.

One of the most important emotions available to the human is *curiosity*. Humans have a desire to know and understand their world, and they wants to understand their place in it. But a conflict arises when "knowledge" interferes with "truth." Knowledge is internal; it is shaped as much by our emotions—many of which have nothing to do with "curiosity"—as by our more abstract intellectual processes. Many of us "know" things that are patently false.

How do we know something is true? For that matter, how do we know something is false? Without putting humanity on some kind of pedestal, why should we believe that the things we "know" to be true are *actu-*

---

[13] Nida, Eugene. Customs and Cultures. William Carey. 1954. 227

ally true, when we each are missing so many of the individual pieces of life's great puzzle?

Being human involves intellectual evolution. Being able to go from the "clean slate" with which we are born to being a quoted doctor of the arts is one of the charms of human intuitiveness. Humans learn; some learn more than others. Early humans understood this and they set up hierarchal social systems. Humans made governments to sustain morality and promote his own well being. Humans have made this system more complicated than it was ever intended to be. Humans throughout the centuries have sought greater power for themselves and greater meaning in their existence, and the apparatus of social organization has grown in complexity beyond our most astute thinkers' ability to apprehend it. Human life now moves in discernible patterns from culture to culture; people live and die by their schools, jobs, religions, governments, clubs and sports.

These institutions train and prepare humans for advancement in life. "Advancement" can be described as "fulfillment," whether that fulfillment is monetary, intellectual, spiritual or social. Such advancement keeps humanity busy and enjoying itself, but it is very much divorced from the kinds of fundamental needs such social systems were originally created to meet.

Humans are defined by these systems, and these systems groom him to function more effectively within these systems. Even dissidents and libertines live and die within their dominion, and they do so happily. Such systems are the only game in town.

What is "true" is a complicated issue to address within such a flowery framework. For both practical and intellectual purposes, a propositional understanding will do, and within this context, a good propositional truth must be equal to the three criteria of truth. The first is that it must correspond with apparent reality, and come equipped with justification, or proof. Second, a truth must have cohesion, or consistency. Finally, the truth must be pragmatic—it must be useful, if only in making predictions about other phenomena. If a proposition lacks one or more of these features, one can proclaim the proposition is false.

The human mind does have boundaries, both skeletal and ectoplasmic, though the average human seldom feels constrained by them. He dwells in the world he has come to know, living a quotidian lifestyle armed with his body (his physical extension) and his mind (his organ or "weapon" that lets him turn ideas into reality, and experience that reality).

> "Our minds are complex fabrics, woven from many different strands and incorporating many different designs. Some of these elements are as old as life itself and others are as new as today's technology. Our minds are just like the minds of other animals in many respects and utterly unlike them in others. An evolutionary

> perspective can help us see how and why these elements of minds came to take on the shapes they have, but no single straight run through time, "from microbes to man," will reveal the moment of arrival of each new thread. So in what follows I have had to weave back and forth between simple and complex minds, reaching back again and again for themes that must be added, until eventually we arrive at something that is recognizably a human mind. Then we can look back, one more time, to survey the differences encountered and assess some of their implications." [14]

The human is rational but adheres to irrational beliefs (God being only the most famous) which severely damage the human's apprehension of truth, but which provide him with a means of living life in a zone of comfort. Rationality is further compromised when greed enters the picture, or any other emotion that demands an excess of predation. But it happens so often—we cannot live rationally, and even when we try, our efforts are thwarted when we come in contact with irrational individuals, or situations that necessitate a powerful emotional response. With that in mind, I ask you to think through the following scenarios. These problems, taken seriously, should lead to some moral searching.

---

[14] Dennett, Daniel C. Kinds of Minds: Toward an Understanding of Consciousness. Basic. New York. 1996

Stranger / Dog Paradox

Imagine you are walking by a river. In that river, two beings are drowning. One is a human stranger—you do not know this person. The other being is your dog, whom you have owned and loved for many years. You only have time to save one or the other. Which will it be?

Most people would like to say that they would save the human stranger, because humans are more precious than canines. Is that true, though? Isn't that a simple human bias? Whether it is or not, one might have trouble living his life, thinking that he sacrificed his beloved dog for someone who may go into the world and kill, murder, rape, and steal.

Be that as it may, most people will still save the human stranger. Let's go to the next question, which is trickier:

Mother / Wife Paradox

In this case you have the same river, but now it is your mother and your wife who are drowning. If you only have the time to rescue one, which will it be?

In evaluating this question, it is necessary to think about certain factors (should this situation arise, you will be forgiven if you fail to think it through in its entirety). First, we can ask ourselves if a blood relationship is more important than an advanced social relationship. Next, we can ask ourselves about the difference in attachment and sentiment between these two people, and how they have shaped our lives. Finally, we can ask ourselves about the value of youth—your mother, after all, has already lived a great deal, whereas your spouse is likely much younger.

These questions have no real answer, because the answers will always vary due to individual circumstances. Nonetheless, it is important to realize the fundamental irrationality of the human and how very pervasive is subjectivity. In our most defining moments, we are seldom rational. In our most defining moments, the concept of "rationality" can seem the most irrational of all.

CHAPTER 4:

INDIVIDUALITY

Were there other minds in the world? Or was Sam the only real thinking being, playing a game with human-shaped machines, designed to stimulate him? Sam was discovering that he could only think for himself—the world's other minds, if such things existed, were closed to him. Sam was lonely.

But what if he could predict the behaviors of those around him? What would that mean? For Sam suspected that, if he were to hurt someone, they would feel pain. If he were to love someone, then they might love him back. Sam worried that if he behaved foolishly, others would observe him.

This, then, was how he was going to invent his new guise and declare his individuality, judging himself by his reflection in a sea of alien faces. He would taste the world and try every approach, approach situations from every angle, until he discovered something that worked. Could Samuel own his world? Could he rule over the minds of his fellow humans—minds he was unsure existed in the first place?

Samuel schemed. He wished the world to bend at his command. He was suddenly greedy. He would make the most of this sad existence, in which his desires were so much greater than his means. He would enjoy himself, if he could, and surround himself with enough noise and distraction to blot out another, terrible reality, which was rapidly dawning on him. That reality was this:

He hated being human.

The humanoid always lives in the present. The present, obviously, is the bridge between the past (where he has been and who he was) and the future (where he will go and who he will be). The present is the result of the past, and it will ultimately result in the future. In the present, man primarily acts according to context, not culture. This is posited and explained in theories like Goffman's Dramaturgical Theory.

The human has made an environment in which he can turn his labor into items of tangibility. The human has the magic ability to turn the intangible tangible (so does the beaver). The results of human labor constitute the majority of humanity's possessions. They began as ideas, transformed into commodities, and now they are bought, sold, and bartered. These items are then sometimes used beyond their intended practical contexts, and are valued for sentimental reasons. When the human observes the world, he is generally unable to apprehend the notion that all he sees is, in some way or another, the product of human thought. His car, his house, his clothes, his gadgets. All inspired within. and created by, the human.

Humans are a peculiar species, with respect to the idea of individualism. No other species aspires towards individuality. We do not see lions painting their fur with Manic Panic hair dye because they want to express themselves. Humans are, at the dawn of the 21st century, almost cartoonishly individualistic. And, somehow, our habit of identity-creation provides us with the sense of security that our abstracted thought-processes would otherwise take away.

We, as humans, exist in a reality where only individual issues matter: Who will benefit from what, and how? We create patterns in our lives that establish our identities and make it easier for us to cope with existential angst. Order is no longer an idea, but a constructed reality inhabited by nearly everyone on earth. Our patterns make our lives predictable and tolerable—just as they make notions like "autonomy" and "freedom" meaningless. So long as we can get our four dollar cup of coffee in the morning, we don't worry whether tomorrow will ever come, and we certainly don't worry about what we'll do with it when it arrives.

So, for the time being—in the "present"—we are "content," just as in the past we were "content" . . . but what happens when our habits become obsolete, and the things from which we once derived comfort and meaning reveal themselves to be chains?

"Purity" is now just an idea. Our concept of good is only defined to the extent that we know evil, and our values are in increasingly rapid flux. The human invests time in himself, and like any investor, his fortunes prosper and slump according to factors he can only dimly comprehend. The things that make us happy today will have unforeseen consequences tomorrow.

Man is only that to himself

This idea of what it means to be human, what it means to be a man and to follow in the footsteps of humankind, are issues relevant only to men. The idea of "man" only exists in the minds of men, and men define their own values.

Man is not "man" to dogs. He is the only one who knows about his own human nature, and he accepts his vague understanding of that nature as natural fact.

Man plans, and creates lasting change in his environment, because man dreams that he might do so.

For man, dreams are fanciful psychological syntheses in which the individual envisions himself with his desires fulfilled. They are the vehicle in which man escapes the dissolute boredom of his daily grind, and imagines that things might be better. *Maybe if I attach one of these to one of those, and then coat the doohicky with adhesive, and then plug it in . . .*

Chapter 5:

Life

Sam was getting twisted. He'd tried to fake his death once before, but the pretty spectacle was ruined when he started laughing while his father recited his eulogy. You should have seen the mourner's faces when they heard giggling coming from inside the coffin. The men threw up and the women clawed at their throats, and everywhere there was a desperate howling. This only made Sam laugh harder.

The funeral home decided to keep their money, but everyone agreed that Sam was lucky not to be in jail. Sam was apathetic when the legal threats were made—he knew that no laws applied to him. He had survived an autopsy, after all: Anything after that was pure fun.

What a day it was.

Samuel bought a dog. A living, breathing animal, it seemed to have no idea it existed, or what it meant to exist. The dog seemed to react to positive and negative stimulus in appropriate ways, but that seemed the extent of its understanding. And all Sam knew was that he liked the dog's company, because it made him feel good. He guessed that was what they called "unconditional love".

When Sam put the dog in its cage, he realized that the dog's life neatly paralleled his own. Sam was a dog, locked up in society and bound by its restraints. Laws were enforced with negative stimuli, and rewards were given to Sam and others when they performed well. *Good humans.*

For a moment, Sam *was* society, hemming the dog in. It was a good feeling, but like so many good feelings, it was lonely.

Sam could reach out and touch and know what it meant to feel the cold metal bars that separated him from ultimate freedom. It was a human invention—the bars, but not the restraints. Did God create Sam to be free? And if he didn't, then why was he created to value freedom so highly? It was a bad situation. But at least Sam had a dog.

. . . and then, there is this thing called life. We make value judgments about it, and create a culture which values human heartbeats and breaths over anything else—it is *homocentric*. But what's the point? Is human life more valuable than that of any other creature? Are humans designed to keep digging and digging, building mental foundations upon which to build artificial meanings to justify our presence? Sure. It's the only game in town. We govern life, through social systems constructed of rules, regulations, and "basic rights."

The human is born into a world that has developed from thoughts, reactions, and interactions, all of which have unknown and unknowable effects upon our behavior and destiny. Despite the obvious gaps in his knowledge, man has sought to make an environment more suited to his needs than the needs of any other living thing. Man cares for himself, and he does so no matter what social forces change through time.

Early humans were too naïve to understand their own nature, or that of the world around them. Religion was an important factor in developing our conception of the human spirit, and was used to provide answers to some of life's toughest questions. An ideal of perfection was established—God—and languages were generated by our need to convey concepts. Passing ideas from one agent to another was important, and enabled us to convey, tentatively at first, the abstracts that we so loved to ponder.

Although human life has flourished based on the traditional principles of religion (as well as "in spite" of the traditional principles of religion: We must remember that the Papacy has, over the centuries, held sway over more deaths than Hitler could ever have hoped to), we have come to a critical time in our evolution. We now must ask: "Is religion relevant to modern man?" With constant, paradigm-shattering, provable advances in the sciences, which provide hard answers to hard questions, the human animal is detaching from its superstitions. But religion did something more than science has thus far attempted. Religion provided hope, inspiration, leadership, community organization and guidelines for a productive way of life—all of which were beneficial to the individual, and to the societies comprised of individuals. Man enters a covenant or contract with the idea of a God, agreeing to live his life in a particular way. Science must provide some kind of substitute for that contract, in order to fully and effectively take the place of now-outmoded religion.

Early, pre-scientific man sought explanations for phenomena that he could not comprehend: "What happens to the sun at night?" or "Why does it rain?" or "I just got hit by lightening—what the fuck was that?"

These questions received fictional answers, which satisfied man's curiosity. Societies began to spread their explanations in the form of stories and myths, which personified nature, and ascribe divine characteristics to the natural world. As these stories became more ornate over the millennia, pantheism gave way to animism and animism gave way to polytheism and polytheism gave way to monotheism: The belief in one God (it was a lot easier for people to remember one God).

And although western science has jeopardized the integrity of religious doctrines, we notice that many people pay little attention to the increasing irrelevance of their most cherished beliefs—they say, "you've gotta take it on *faith*." Maybe they're right, although scientists would disagree.

Religion is under attack, especially in the western world. Sanctity has been de-glorified and made into a commodity of sorts, purchased with the altruism of its congregants. As the plaudit sounds from the followers, their pockets are emptied into the donations box. But why?

Money made the human compete, struggle and survive in a way completely foreign to the vast majority of man's million-year history. The human has to produce in society in order to ensure his own survival. The human relies on commodities, and this has ironically made him a commodity to the producers. Those who sit at the crux of the social pyramid and dictate the social forces say one thing, and one thing only: *Consume.*

For man believes that the received materialist ideology—which he does not recognize as being a "received" ideology at all—will automatically create "happiness" and "fulfillment" the moment materialist wishes are granted. It is in this relationship that something special happens: The human is turned into a commodity. The slave turns from human to machine. He is the meat machine that tends to the needs of this other red-blooded creature—the original commodity—and this situation only exists by virtue of the socially constructed understandings of the world that man has created for himself to live by. He uses excuses such as: "This is the way the Bible tells me to live," or "I am predisposed to be smarter than you, so it is only right that I take advantages of your strengths."

Does that make money evil? Is money to blame for the loss of human individuality? Or can an economic foundation be said to be the incentive for individual aspirations? This duality or modern social life exhibits man as a mouse contemplating a trap, stuck choosing between cheese and life. If the rat doesn't eat the cheese he starves, and if the rat goes for the cheese, a cold metal bar will snap on his neck.

George Wilhelm Fredrich Hegel, Karl Marx and Frederich Engles understood the economy as the foundation of social life. The idea of *dialectical materialism* seeks to identify the human, and identify the exact point in human interaction at which there becomes a need for "prosperity." Classes of people are born, and the human has been taken from his natural, animalistic state and made into something else, something different, that science cannot explain. Opposed classes breed new economic factions through old class antagonisms.

Classes of people living together created a whole new dimension to our understanding of the way humans interact and live on a macro level. Social theories begot commonage lifestyles and ways to set up complex social organizations. For example, Utilitarianism seeks to create the greatest good for the greatest amount of people. While this sounds good, it rests on sophist grounds. Utilitarianism falsely gives its followers the sense that it wants to preserve the human community but at the same time it recognizes little or no value in life. In a strict utilitarian mindset, it would be perfectly acceptable to do *anything* as long as it brings happiness to many. This social system lacks consideration for any number of minorities—and, indeed, fails to recognize basic disparities between human beings, failing, as it were, to see the forest for the trees.

A paradox occurs when analyzing the economic foundation of human societies. Capitalism advocates free thought and the pursuit of individuality, and rewards those who excel as individuals. Fascism, Nazism, socialism, communism and Marxism disable or put the human at a disadvantage in the development of his individual will. In these mechanistic systems, the human has no identity: He is a worker, a bureaucrat, or a slave to the system that he is forced to adhere to. Resistance results in the killing of the person (I do not say "individual," because in these systems, there is no individual), and what you have read prior and will read after this proposition simply couldn't make any difference to your life as lived under such conditions. No self-assertion—be it in the reading of a book, in the viewing of a film, or in the collection of small and meaningful moments that comprise the life of the individual—makes one whit of difference. Even in these systems, the human is a commodity. They lack any consideration of human worth. Why? Are humans really, truly disposable?

Here, once again, money is the determining force that guides human endeavor. In modern society, it is rare that the individual prospers for anything but his selfish interests, and prosperity is never, ever divorced from money.

This is where the essence of experience becomes lost and transubstantiated into representationalism. This doesn't happen with any other animal. Only amongst humans can life, in its totality, be represented monetarily—and only amongst humans can direct experience be replaced with symbols. Man created such a system arbitrarily, and has now become so accustomed to living by it that any alternative existence seems preposterous. Man creates his own accommodations blindly, and then claims to need them.

Technology is one such accommodation. Scholars like Daniel Dennett posit that there are "different ways of cognitive thinking" for the individual— such as knowing and assuming. Assumptions represent what the human mind believes "is supposed to happen," and modern technology has caused man to rely on more, and more elaborate, assumptions than his ancestors did. Modern technology—and especially "luxury technology"—is one of those "blind accommodations" that man, or *the concept of man*, relies on to make his every-day existence manageable. He creates a comfort zone, a sphere of experience that is amenable to *his* individual needs.

This comfort zone still creates a distortion of what the human actually *is*, confusing his fundamental condition with what we imagine that condition to be. Even in their current state of high development, humans still often verbally acknowledge their own animalistic, cthonian nature—and this may be one of the most accurate *knowings* that man can attain whilst analyzing the human. The quest to understand that animalistic nature is at the root of much human intellectual endeavor, although the reconciliation of the animalistic urges of the brain's R-complex and limbic systems with its highly-evolved neo-cortex, from whence sprang civilization, may prove ultimately impossible.

Humanity's technological comfort-zone—which exists, in part, to insulate man from his animalistic nature—has short-circuited the traditional process of Darwinian natural selection. Now, rather than species succeeding or failing based upon their biological adaptations to their environment, man has, through strength of will and intellect, forced his environment to conform to him. It is possible that mankind has, through the creation of such insulation, obfuscated his true identity and sublimated some of his most salient, truest traits. It is probable that we will never know if this is true or false.

Changing the subject slightly, there is one final idea that I would like to go over as we reach the conclusion of this chapter: Man and his emotions.

Did man create emotion, and if not, then where and how did these phenomena arise? When we talk about emotion, we mean the physical bodily processes that lead to abstract feelings. And when we try to convey our sense of individual feeling from one agent to another, there is a false sense of actually *knowing* that our communication has been successful. As with the human understanding of color, there is no guarantee that any two people process emotions similarly. It would be foolish to suppose that a man can actually love in the same way as his fellow man. In the name of lingual expediency, we fall subject to hasty generalizations that presuppose that all men experience things similarly.

There is certainly some consistency in man's emotional motivation—he seeks to have intimate relationships for the protection of his own insecurities, and he uses intimate relationships to satisfy longings that were set forth in the beginning of his biology. All men appear to dramatize the conscious pursuit of such satisfaction with emotion.

Man created his particular sense of sentimentalism, and in doing so, calcified his own self-image. It was in the metajuxtaposition of himself upon his environment that he gained a sense of himself—identity, defined by contrasts. Whether he will one day actually *know*, factually, who he is, has yet to be determined.

Philosophy and art throughout history—this book included—exists, at least partly, to offer man a glimpse of an over-arching rationale that exists behind the turbulent maelstrom of his emotions. Despite the consistency of this fascination, little thought has been devoted to questioning why humans are so fascinated by their own, hidden motivations.

CHAPTER 6:

A MEANING OF THE WORLD AROUND HIM

He could feel his heart beating but didn't know why. The blood surged through his veins. He felt like a big, wet, mechanical clock. His body was programmed to perform in a certain way—to keep Sam alive, to act in his best interest, to be the hedonistic savage that he was.

Samuel was beginning to see the dichotomy that was his existence. Surely his body could operate on it's own, but without Sam there, it would be pointless. Sam wondered if maybe it wasn't pointless, anyway.

We come now to The *Meaning* of Life. We could approach this by asking the same clichéd existential questions, such as: What's the point to being human? *Is*

there a point to being a human? We won't attack these questions this way.

In the creation of the cosmos, where does man fit in? Is he an explorer? Is he a slave? Or rather, is he just a delusional animal, cursed with the false pretense that he actually stands a chance of understanding anything at all?

Man is doomed by the notion of free will. It is an albatross. He will never know if he is truly a "free" being or not. In fact, philosophical thought has long undermined the assumption of man's actual freedom, as has science. Over the last hundred years, science has devoted a large part of its inquiry into understanding the physical realities of the human neurological processes.

Traditionally, the argument against the notion of free will is predicated upon scientific theory. There is a causal relation between the events that occur in the world. Everything has a preceding event and every proceeding event has an antecedent. Initially, the presupposition rests on the basis that the formation of the cosmos created an inescapable chain of events: This school of thought has been labeled "determinism."

On the molecular level, this seems to be how it goes. One can find that the body is composed of tiny molecular components, all of which are governed by natural laws. This is typical of all macro-atomic objects. From the human perspective, thoughts cause actions ("making decisions"), and these thoughts are nothing more than tiny synaptic bursts of electricity. Those synaptic actions are obviously physical, physics-governed objects, doing their thing. It is safe to say that these atoms are governed by the same natural laws that govern all physical behavior—the actions of which those tiny objects cannot deviate.

So, where did the notion of free will go? Philosophically and biologically, it has been disproved (at least as we typically understand it—there are some yahoos out there on the rugged epistemological terrain who claim that determinism does not detract from free will, but they are playing a semantics game, and they are hopelessly inbred). Theology is the only remaining field of thought still seriously preaching the idea that humans are empowered with genuine decision-making tools. But even here, there is a paradox.

From religion, we come to know God as Omnipotent, Omnibenevolent, and, most crucially, Omniscient (all-knowing). But, if God is all-knowing, than how could a human possibly have free will? How can he truly make "choices" if the big guy in the sky already knows the decisions that the human is going to make, as well as their ultimate outcomes?

Aquinas thought about this a lot, and so did Calvin. Pope Benedict XVI probably does not.

Desperately, we see that man is no more than a puppet, an animal, a loose marble rolling down a steep hill. What to do with this hideous creature?

FUN THINGS TO DO WITH HUMAN MEAT-PUPPETS

1. He can be kept content if he is given the knowledge of an ever-loving God watching over him. He is more emotionally stable when he actually believes he is in control of his life. Abstract denials of his decision-making apparatus compromise his very existence, and so he prefers to go to sleep every night with a feeling of control. Control is just a happy illusion, preventing man from drowning in the tragedy that is his existence. In the final analysis, man is left with little hope—only the hope he is given, and which he has no choice but to accept. This is how fate would have it.
2. I cannot speak from personal experience, but my sensai tells me that it's fun to kick-box with women in the third trimesters of their pregnancies.
3. Pogoing at church.
4. Looking through old photo albums and trying to link yourself, mentally, with the retarded-looking five year old playing with the hose in the front yard.

5. Actually, there are only about four worthwhile things to do with human meat-puppets.
6. Oh! I thought of a good one for "number 5!" How's about "Writing A Book On Existentialism?"
7. Right. And some people say that the sixth most entertaining thing to do with human meat-puppets is trying to get them to let you Take Over The World.

We have seen that free will is a myth, a device used to keep humankind comfy and dumb. The next question then becomes: What about man's agenda? Does he have one? And if he does, is it valid, as he did not create it of his own volition? Or—and this is a seductive idea—does it come from a Higher Source?

If the latter is true and it isn't, man is seen as God's worker. He is just another machine, another tool to accomplish an end that he will never see and will never be given Ultimate Cosmic Credit for. He then becomes an ant, moved by nature to fill a specific role.

Humanity's freedom has been taken away, and without it he is helpless and at sea, with no rescue boat and no life preserver in sight. Waiting for the inevitable, and waiting for his demise, separated from it by unknowable amounts of random randomness. And so what?

But, in our attempt to understand the human more thoroughly, let's exercise our options outside the milieu of free will. Striking this from our equations, save when necessary, will provide insight into the depths of human rationality, and human imperfections.

It can be said that the social attributes of man make this anatomical machine imperfect. Societal conditioning causes weakness by giving man an unnecessary and counter-productive despairing outlook, and pervert his mind with irrational thoughts on topological thinking levels, which distract the homo faber.

The human is nothing but a clock. A faux-autonomous machine, the human heart analogous to a self-winding spring. Both are wound from the beginning, and both stop ticking in the end.

The sheer mechanism of his condition devalues man, and strips him of his sense of belonging to the human community. These points may be moot, as, with respect to the above writings, we have come to understand that man really has little or no choice in the grand scheme of things. This makes the concept "responsibility" meaningless. And if man is not responsible for his actions, or the choices for which he is punished or rewarded, then who is?

"Morality" starts seeming a little archaic, here. Evil and goodness morph into a single category, "action," and the notion of subjective value is destroyed. These thoughts, although philosophical, begin to dispel humanity's most vaunted historic approaches to social interaction and organization. The power of the human spirit is demolished instantaneously; noble and nefarious endeavors become erased, and The Great God Objectivity cackles wildly at the flimsy construction of human innovation.

The Great God Objectivity: You can't take responsibility for any of these creations.

Human Nature: Why not?

TGGO: Because you *had* to do these things, despite your belief that you did them of your own volition. These things were destined before you even dreamed they were possible. It was all bound to happen. I'm sorry, but you simply had no choice.

HN: I feel so used. I feel like a machine, or at best, an extremely low-rent hooker.

TGGO: Stop talking and get back to work.

HN: Cocksucker.

TGGO: I knew you'd say that.

The human is a form of ideological Play-Doh: It is objectified, personified, deified, criminalized, and in some countries circumsized at the whim of blind, terrible nature.

Human values are not abstract notions. They are, however, good guides to living what we deem a "decent" lifestyle. The human ideology of "core values" that permeates western thought is comprised of manmade ideals, which have found their most eloquent expressions in religion.

People do posses a feeling of "a priori rights," such as the sustenance and nurturing of his own life, and the equally-important right of the individual to think for himself. And while this may lead to the human living a socially acceptable lifestyle, it also imposes the same value system we got rid of previously—by substituting freedom with nature.

CHAPTER 7:

HE WHO BELIEVED IN AN IDEA OF TIME

He wasn't human anymore. He was no more and no less alive than any other object he had ever encountered. His sense of control was gone, and he felt like an exile from the human community. He could not belong to a community that was living in such rank dishonesty. He didn't want to be a part of the moral fabric that man had made for himself. Sam was alone, and the more alive he felt, the deader he was to the world, and it to him. He could look at people from a distance and analyze their very belief systems, destroy them, and then rebuild them with whatever notion he felt like contriving on the spot.

To Sam, Time was more than a numerical expression: It was a story. Sam was the narrator, and no one was going to stop him.

The clock's hands ticked past each other. The big hand had a job to do, and there was little that could prevent it from completing its task. The clock had no need to be wound: It was automatic, possessed of a self-winding principle that acted upon the intentional or unintentional energy of what it is attached to (in this case, a human).

It was time for the second hand to swoop past both the hour indicator and the minute reminder—they waved at each other because it was a brief visit, like all the others, and so a wave was all that was necessary. They knew that they would see each under similar circumstances in just a moment. All the hands (second, minute, hour) had jobs to do, and so long as their body was healthy, that job would get done. They all shared that body, and their functions were inter-related and dependent upon one another, whether they knew it or not.

They couldn't care less who was watching, or what was going on beyond the crystal dome above them. All they knew was duty. And even if they didn't understand the higher meaning of their duty, it didn't matter—they would do it anyway. They didn't know what else to do. The crystal dome was nothing more than a protection, so as to ensure that the hands would not be disturbed. They didn't want distraction. They were uninterested in crime, rape, love, happiness, sadness, death, politics, canasta or anything else. Those were all independent concepts, encompassed and defined by the ebb and flow of time (the very element the clock was representing). If humanity stopped breathing tomorrow, the clock would still have to do its job.

The gears smoothly enveloped each other and all the mechanisms were perfectly predictable. They were symbols, representations of a part of reality discovered by humans that functions in accordance with obvious, logical, natural law. There were tiny rivets, and each felt the tension of the gears.

Sam had believed that Time was only a concept until recently. Then he discovered it was real, and inseparable from the fabric of his reality. Time was an immaterial force with a physical influence, and a proportional metric to the speed of light. Science was fucking with The Fundaments, and certainties were uncertain.

The clock is an object, a symbol, and an instrument of measurement. One could say that it measures reality. It is a mechanistic, independent society, in which all the parts must, can, and do work together.

No moment is ever the same as any other, and each nanosecond is independent within it. Its life is its own. It is that nanosecond's exclusive niche, and no other nanosecond could have filled it. Time is a mystical continuum, which defies rational exegeses, but which operates by knowable (and increasingly known) laws to produce the past and ring in the relative darkness of the future.

Ultimately, what would the world be like without time? Only by forgetting about a moment's alienation from all other moments can we view life as it is: A canvas splattered with an elaborate action painting of blended emotions, situations, and aspirations.

The clock is as alive as we. The clock and the human. Circadian rhythm, heartbeats and the pulse of the second all aspire to the Next and relinquish the Last. There certainly are elements which divide the clock from the human, and it should be understood that there are vastly more dissimilarities than there are similarities—though there are a great many of those, and the more you think about it, the greater their number. One similarity, however, dwarves all other considerations in importance:

The watch is no less *alive* than man.

A Brief Digression

Hey! I just thought of a funny joke!

Alright. I hope I get it right. I mean, I heard it once, and I think I remember it, but I get nervous around crowds. Uh. Cool. Right. Check it out:

Um, a college student was showing off his new apartment to a few friends. His friends were oohing and aahing appropriately.

The Clock That Told More Than Time

"And this is my bedroom," said the college student, ushering them into a room full of pizza boxes and used condoms. In the middle of the room, for no obvious reason, there sat a big, bronze gong and ball-peen hammer.

"Hey," said one of his friends, "What's with the gong?"

"Oh," said the student, "It's my Talking Clock."

"A Talking Clock? What in the ever-loving shit is a Talking Clock?"

"Watch," said the college student, and he proceeded to smack the gong with the ball-peen hammer. There was a shocking crash, and a moment of silence.

And then, from beyond the bedroom wall, there came the voice of the student's neighbor: *"What the fuck are you doing? It's two in the fucking morning!"*

Ha ha ha. That joke gets me laid a lot. It really *eases* the *existential angst*, you know?

End of Digression

Men are not so different from clocks. The society that man created, and in which he lives, operates according to its structure like the gears of a clock. Both are "poetry in motion," if you're romantically inclined, and both are "dead," if you're not.

Man is the first watch to make sense of its dreams, and the first to fall prey to dreaming's attendant psycho-semantic obsessions. The humans of today are not the same as the humans of one hundred years ago. The old humanity was vastly more self-sufficient: Today's human is dependent upon elements of a mechanistic society that are owned and operated at a great remove from wherever he performs his daily labor. He lives in a machine world, in which it is easy to forget how much of his daily life is removed from animal-nature, and dependent upon the manifestation of man's imagination and will to create. The light is shut off, and he lives in the dark world of the machine, in which man's nature is imprisoned behind a pall of wire and steel. The human is no longer the architect of his life—the machine has eased his burdens. Man is now reliant upon the machinations of a world that was created from the dreams and wishes of his forebears, the precepts of which he has no choice but to accept, for the sake of convenience.

And there is the problem: When man relies so strongly upon the machine, he is robbing himself of life's highest expression and fulfillment. When man sits in front of a television, he is watching other people live more intensely than he is affording himself an opportunity to. When the television is removed from his life, he has been deprived of the very special tool the human needs to understand, and accept, the world

---

[15] TV B-Gone Pamphlet- Marvelous little device. www.tvbgone.com

around him—an extended family of known and knowable human beings. "All those things you wanted to have in your life: passion, romance, love, childhood, parenthood, adventure . . . when are you going to do all that?"[15]

> People on TV are not your friends. They're not in the room with you. You are alone in the dark, staring at a plastic box. Think about it. This is like a science fiction horror story; but it's really happening. People have stopped living as humans and connected themselves to machines instead . . . You're only going to live for 75 years, if you're lucky. How much time do you have left? Enough to spend one whole day every week with fake friends, watching their imitation lives instead of living your own?

> The Average American watches 4.5 hours of television every day. You sleep for eight hours. You get up and work for eight hours. Come home, eat some dinner and turn on the television. A few hours later you're getting sleepy. Time for bed. On your deathbed, what if someone could give you back those ten years of television? What if they said you could have another ten years to be with the people you love, find new people, do things differently? What would you say?[16]

---

[16] Ibid, www.whitedot.org

CHAPTER 8:

Nihilism and Adaptation: Fun Suggestions for Saturday Night

Sam was content with the idea of *nothing*. *Nothing* was significant, and *nothing* but. The future meant *nothing* to him, anymore. He had been to the event horizon of breathing life; he had looked deep into the black hole of despair, and now he cheerfully accepted his fate within it.

Realizations like those are sad and solemn for many. For Sam, it was moment in which he caught a glimpse of a higher truth about himself, and his fellow human beings. Those around him didn't understand why he saw despair as a good thing. And, in truth, he never had. Rather, he saw it is a more truthful way of dealing with existence: one that captured human dignity without lying.

It was shortly after his departure from reality that Sam encountered one of the most exquisite juxtapositions in life.

He was walking along the midway when it happened. He could hear the sounds of seagulls, and he wasn't thinking about much else. He liked the sounds of the seagulls. They reminded him of clocks.

There was an old derelict crouching not to far from where Sam was walking. He was resting on the balls of his feet, wrapped up in blue blankets. They looked like they had been expensive, at one time or another. Sam wondered who had bought them, and what beds they had graced before they found their way here, fraying on the splintered midway boards.

The derelict glanced upwards, and for a moment his eyes met Sam's. They were blue, like his blankets—and then, they were not eyes anymore. For the briefest of instants, they were portals to a place far beyond the here and now, and distance, doubt and dereliction were smashed within them. Love, trust, hatred, envy, and pity all screamed through the optic channel. Thoughts, feelings—a true empathy in a blaze of inexplicable communion . . . and then they were eyes again, and they were looking at something else, scanning the sea foam for things that Sam couldn't begin to guess at.

Do abstract concepts really exist, or are they mere intellectual inventions created by man? Philosophical social criticisms exist for historical analysis on contemporary humankind. Nihilism, while seen as negative, can help to provide the means for a more productive society. Is the concept of God a man made idea?

Does it all really matter? Everything? All of it? The nihilist would say it doesn't, and unfortunately, that is as far from a pragmatic view as one can get. Could we be apathetic about nihilism? Yes! But fortunately, even the most nihilistic among us can still recognize values, even if we doubt their ultimate worth. And without the nihilistic impulse, it is demonstrably easy for man to get caught up in the glory of his own arbitrary abstractions, assigning ultimate value to imaginary objects, and judging the real by the yardstick of the dream. It is therefore necessary for nihilism to exist, in order to allow man to see the gray, in between the colors of the grass and sky.

The world's got too much sentimental *stuff* in it for us to care as much as we'd like to—you cannot cry for every hungry child. The other side of the coin is that to live with no empathy or dreams and submit to life's ultimate meaninglessness is to be a deeply wretched person. The human cannot walk this road, and thus his manic urgency to develop abstractions to fill his life.

Most of the things that human beings invite into their lives are imported based upon the glimmering, distant hope of future satisfaction. Intellectually, the human has assessed the idea of being *human in a habitat*, and has thusly fomented his necessity for such. And so on and so forth.

The human is ultimately ignorant. He has created theories that posit "feasible" explanations for the order of things. Scientific theories, often in conflict with theological considerations, offer different suggestions as to the nature of motion's antecedent—"The Prime Mover." Both science and theology look to answer this question, but only science can offer empirical evidence in support of its conclusions. Somehow, though, both seem necessary within their contexts.

If we accept that life is one long chain of events, then is it not appropriate to ask questions like:

When did motion start?

When did life start?

Do concepts exist only because we have language?

What got them started?

What was the magic that gave man the inspiration to be the architect of his own dreams?

When does a human become *human*?

Although I admittedly neglect speculating on the nature of consciousness, it is a good idea to ask questions about the nature of man's thought processes. "Apperception" is man's ability to realize himself, and it is a common ability amongst all humans. But while he may be aware of himself and his surroundings, he is almost universally ignorant of the very genius he possesses. Born intelligent, he is blind to the mystery of intelligence.

Man is the ultimate goal-creator. He empirically observes his surroundings and creates hypotheses about the likely outcomes of various actions, and then acts accordingly—though, as we saw earlier, no choice is involved. It appears that Nature is governing all of human industry. If nature governs man's thoughts and actions, then it can also be said that nature relieves man's burden of responsibility.

And it can be said that, thanks to nature's omnipotence, man's goals are ultimately meaningless. They are fanciful creations that keep his spirit happy, and create a palisade between him and the brute realities of his world. Goals are abstract constructions, allowing man to deal with his everyday situations and assert a fragile order onto a chaotic world. As in Eden, man is the Great Namer. Adam was the first taxonomist, and we are all his descendents.

Man the Thinker, Man the Do-er, Man the Creator, Man the Creature. In all his roles, his only worth is that which he creates for himself. Given the enormity of the cosmos, it is foolish to suppose that worth might come from any higher, intelligent source. If it did, we would probably all be made in the perfect Image of God.

Imago Dei. If humans are created in the image of God, then why are we fallible? Why are we in a constant state of evolution, and subject to mutation?

Man is created in many forms. Why? These inherent differences breed diversity, but they also give rise to bias. There is nothing man can do to overcome the differences that he is born with. The immediate and obvious answer is obviously cosmetic reconstruction. Our poster-child is none other than Anti-Human Michael Jackson. Jackson has spent more money on cosmetic surgery than most CEOs will make in a lifetime. Jackson seeks to alter his physicality because of social and psychological forces, and the problems almost certainly go deeper than one would expect. The modern (western) human wishes to idealize everything that is thrown in front of him. Beauty is the object, and ugliness is the enemy, and the symbol-making process takes notice: That which is beautiful is successful, talented, wealthy, healthy, and symbolic of everything that is good in each passing moment. Such thinking creates ever-larger divides between people, and in a world that preaches unification and cosmopolitanism, the effects are counter-productive.

Man feels comfortable with those who act and look like him. And if that is the emotional support that he needs, then he will stop at nothing to be with his kind. This may or may not be true in every case, but it is important to understand the psychological influences that compel man to commune most comfortably with those like him.

Prejudices and biases only exist because of the natural inequalities that humans are endowed with. Although men are usually created with the same fundamental attributes, men themselves substantially differ from each other. For example, a person who is born with a body that will develop great physical agility might have to exert himself less in the fifty yard dash than a fat kid with a thyroid problem. Ethics are called into questions when Speedy wins the race and Pig Boy had to work twice as hard. The separation of *merit* and *desert* comes to light, here. When human development progressed to the point where man had to look beyond his obvious physical permutations, people attempted to unite, despite looks, and establish a common belief system. Nevertheless, racism is everywhere. "Race" is a point of pride amongst people of all ethnic backgrounds—one that cannot be abolished without the disenfranchisement of individual thought.

Whatever its objective truth, man uses religion as a tool. Among other things, it is a tool to deprive people of their natural inquisitiveness and desire to understand the world around them, and it is a tool to grant the dysfunctional man a foundational excuse for his actions. Man's actions are informed by his dogmas. Symbioses, mutualism and parasitism exist, in part, because of the fictions man has developed to justify them. And whether those actions result in peace or violence, bounty or famine, they have always come about as a result of man's capacity to adapt to changing circumstance.

"Religion is the opium of the masses." - Karl Marx

But what are we really talking about here? The key to understanding the human is in his adaptive abilities, which he uses to exploit the resources around him. He is a vile creature, set to do what has to be done so he can get his way. He will dilute his race, and eventually the only race will be human—culture will be dead. And when humans are raceless, they will soon abandon their creeds and religions bias, and quite possibly their sexuality.

These are the historical and contemporary characteristics that we see man content with. He is on the road to reconciling himself with himself, for good or ill—but his truce with his environment will likely never be anything but uneasy.

"Adaptation" is the key to understanding the human. Man's adaptive abilities are what enable him to cope with a fractured mind and an alienated soul. It could be said that man has done more than simply adapt to his environment—some will say that he has innovated, shown sparks of creative genius or carelessly destroyed things upon which he depends. He has created and destroyed habitats and species, and there is not a square inch of the planet that has not been dramatically impacted, directly or indirectly, by man's endless ministrations. Though it doesn't seem that way, all of this comes under the umbrella of "adaptation." Even things that were ultimately counter-productive—like, say, the way in which the inhabitants of Easter Island demolished all of their domestic food sources—were adaptive in their moment. When the land was dark, man founded fire. When he was hungry he ate. When he was thirsty for knowledge he invented the word.

Chapter 9:
Acclamations of Truth, Untold Lies of the Social Machine

"We live in a jungle of pending disasters, walking constantly across a minefield... will my plane crash tomorrow? What If I miss it? Will the next one crash? Will my house burn down? Gover's friend's house in Topanga burned yesterday, nothing saved except an original Cezanne. Where will it all end?"

-Hunter S. Thompson

It's been a while since Sam gave up on life. He had bourn witness to the world around him. He had witnessed societies built to the sky and razed to the ground. To Sam, life was just a series of disappointments—a failure dogging every triumph. He couldn't handle it any more.

There were things that went on in the human world that he could not submit to, or even tacitly approve of. Corruption, greed, poverty, war, hunger, pain, suffering—these were only a few of Humanity's Greatest Hits, and he couldn't ignore them. As near as Sam could tell, life was far more venal, cheap and corrupt than it was profound, worthy and sacred.

He lived in a world crippled by apathy. He resided in a society that gave acclaim to people who hurt others and lied. They owned the world, and because of it, Sam could never know what it was to be free. Humans were phony. Their values and priorities made Sam want to puke. The nine-to-five job, the family stampeding off to happy hour. It might sound nice, from a particular perspective, but what happens when you get fired? Or when someone in your family dies? Or when you turn into a raving meth junkie? What did a person possess that was uniquely his own, beyond the power of circumstance to snatch away?

Sam resisted the world. He would not become one of those who he hated. Sam schemed to live differently, and in his daily life, did things that others didn't. He took time to think about the world; he did not just let days pass.

Sam resolved to live as a nihilist would, recognizing no inherent value in the world that was keeping him prisoner. It dawned on Sam that the only way to smell freedom would be to unlock his cell by taking his own life. The truth was clear; that the human entity was a prisoner of circumstance.

Those around Sam believed that he had one of those "sicknesses," some kind of social disorder. It was likely true. He was too pure, and he was so crazy that he couldn't stop trying to cleanse himself of the evil that surrounded him.

The social machine's hegemony is heinous. It manifests most powerfully in the interactions of peers. Within society, humans are conditioned at a young age to identify with the social characteristics of peers. Common sense shows us how to distance ourselves from the detriments of such social forces. However, it is impossible to know the precise nature of the dominion of those forces—we cannot know the size and shape of their dark influence.

The human uses intoxicants to help buffer the experiences he encounters in everyday life. These substances that help the human neglect truth and perpetuate an illusory existence that parades itself as reality. This makes truth harder and harder to reach. Reality fades with every sip, puff, injection or snort.

The vagaries of social interaction are to blame for humanity's obsession with distancing itself from truth. Manmade social constructs interfere with humans. It is the masses that dwell in apathy, while the few, the sober (in every sense of the word), search for truth.

Modern man is too influenced by social factors. Eliminating those factors is not necessary. Rather, cultural change may lead to an overall improvement in man's intellectual and emotional comportment. External (social) stimuli affect the internal reactor (man, and his thoughts), which are then projected outward, into the world around him.

The same relationship is present within the mind itself. Subconscious thought influences conscious thought while conscious thought influences the subconscious. The unknown and unknowable intricacies of the genesis of daily, human consciousness cause serious problems when trying to understand what it is to be a conscious person. Some say that the details are unimportant, so long as humanity can create its happy fictions and satisfy its own needs.

Needs? What are those? More fictions. Needs are primitive instinctual drives which, if ignored, will lead to death, pain and suffering. And so what?

Humans are the damndest *hedonists* the planet has wrought from its biosphere—probably because we are so good at getting what we need, and moving on to the more mysterious realm of *what we want*. But with all the supposed understanding of "progress"—what real human accomplishments have been made? Longevity? Who would want to live longer in a world they know nothing about? Putting a man on the moon? We can't even get to the bottom of the Mariana Trench—why are we going to the moon? That damned space race.

All in all, when it is over, life is a myth. Man walks the streets, enamored by the supposed innovations of his fellow man. The streets pity him. The lights shine brightly and man comes to see the light as *truth, happiness,* and *prosperity.*

He opened the door timidly. He didn't know why he was here, or what his purpose was. The concrete was hot, and the humidity was getting to him. Sweat stained his clothes, which felt suddenly too heavy.

Approaching the counter was a pug-ugly little woman. She had the cranial dimensions of a hydrocephalic troglodyte, and her movements and gestures reinforced the image. She was not smiling. She had a job to do, and that was it.

"One ticket please," said the man. There was fear in his voice. He knew he was going to see more than he paid for.

"Fifteen dollars," replied the trog.

He paid his money and stepped through the gates. Black iron bars separated two types of life— the free and the imprisoned.

Organisms, animals, living and breathing creatures banged around, making sounds, noises, gestures. As he approached the monkey cage, he had to dodge flying feces. It reminded him of a homeless man he once saw throwing shit at small children.

It had changed his life. The sounds of children yelling and screaming, overpowered by the laughs of the drunken bindlerstiff. Those events captured emotion. There was something real there, but it was nameless.

There were all types of organisms at the zoo, but one exhibit was troublesome. He had never seen these creatures before. They were bi-pedal, erect animals, possessed of an elegant lust for communication.

"Silly," he thought: "These things remind me of myself."

There were four of them sitting at what appeared to be a table. Two older ones and two younger ones.

As he approached the iron gates, he read the sign:

"Homo Sapien—Sometimes known as 'homo faber'. Dwells in a vast array of environments. Primitive beasts with omnivorous appetites. Homo sapiens are known to construct complex social organizations."

He laughed and walked away, with tears in his eyes.

But *is* man just another caged beast in this world? Is he a product of the bars that confine him and the laws by which he lives? Rousseau once said, "Man is born free, but is everywhere in chains." It's a social sickness that taints man when he becomes aware of his surroundings. Oblivion is not safety. Man remains in the state of the constant, and the constant is not fixed.

Levels of consciousness divide awareness, and it is only by negotiating these levels that man may teeter on the brink of understanding the *animal* that he naturally is. But all of those levels are governed by biological imperatives—they know what they want, and they know when they're not getting it.

Does man have a choice in his reactions? Can he be socialized to respond differently? Ivan Pavlov has shown this to be true. And if responses can be conditioned, aren't they just a set of *constructed* guides for man to live by? If these constructions can be changed, then reality as we know it can be interpreted subjectively, and the fixed, moral fiber that informs our vision of "the good life" begins to fray. Man created the social condition for the life that he lives. He created materialism with his needs and his desires, as he created himself from his fears, and desires inarticulate.

When man became a-perceptive (self aware), he was subtly coming to understand the difference that exists between himself and his environment. This was the holy moment when mankind said, "Do I want to keep living in this goddamned cave, or do I want to rock?" And being that he chose the latter, he constructed a world in which he could be almost unimpeded by violent nature, and then casually, if at all, offer glib explanations for the bifurcations between him and his world.

We live in an age in which man's society and politics are plagued by religions, both recognized and subtle—the social machine of received dogma and easy answers. In the full glory of artificial modernity, man is posing a question to himself: He wants to know if he should live in the world he created, or the one that was already there. Quite a lot hinges on the answer, but most of us are only just beginning to grasp the question. —C.B.F.

Bibliography

Law, Stepthen. *The Philosophy Gym*. St. Martins Press. UK. 2003

Rollins, L.A. . *The Myth of Natural Rights*. Loompanics. Washington. 1983

Fish, Stanley. *There's No Such Thing As Free Speech: And it's a good thing too*. Oxford. New York. 1994

Hartnack, Justus. *Philosophical Problems: A modern introduction*. Humanities. Copenhagen. 1972

Hofstafter, Douglas R. *Godel, Escher, Bach: An eternal golden braid*. Basic. New York. 1979

Debord, Guy. *Society of the Spectacle*. Black & Red. Detroit. 1983

Marx, Karl and Engels, Fredrich. *The Communist Manifesto*. Penguin. London. 1985

Pojman, Louis P. *What can we know? An introduction to the theory of knowledge*. Wadsworth. Connecticut. 2001

Printed in the United States
59616LVS00001B/52-69